THE SOUTHERN QUESTION

PICAS SERIES 46

ANTONIO GRAMSCI

THE SOUTHERN QUESTION

A NEW TRANSLATION AND
AN INTRODUCTION
BY PASQUALE VERDICCHIO

GUERNICA

TORONTO · BUFFALO · CHICAGO · LANCASTER (U.K.)

2009

Antonio D'Alfonso, editor
Guernica Editions Inc.
P.O. Box 117, Station P, Toronto (ON), Canada M5S 2S6
2250 Military Road, Tonawanda, N.Y. 14150-6000 U.S.A.

Distributors:
University of Toronto Press Distribution,
5201 Dufferin Street, Toronto (ON), Canada M3H 5T8
Gazelle Book Services, White Cross Mills, High Town, Lancaster LA1 1XS U.K.
Independent Publishers Group,
814 N. Franklin Street, Chicago, Il. 60610 U.S.A.

Printed in Canada.
Originally published by Bordighera Incorporated (VIA Folios 5) in 1995
First Guernica edition, second printing.

Legal Deposit — Fourth Quarter
Library of Congress Catalog Card Number: 2005931737
Library and Archives Canada Cataloguing in Publication
Gramsci, Antonio, 1891-1937
The southern question / Antonio Gramsci ;
translated by Pasquale Verdicchio.
Translation of: Questione meridionale.
ISBN 978-1-55071-196-7

1. Italy--Politics and government--1922-1945. 2. Italy,
Southern--Politics and government--1922-1945. 3. Italy, Southern-
Economic conditions. I. Verdicchio, Pasquale, 1954- II. Title.
DG828.G7213 2005   945.091   C2005-905217-1

Contents

Introduction

Antonio Gramsci's *Notes on the Southern Problem and on the Attitudes Toward It of Communists, Socialists and Democrats* was penned shortly before his imprisonment at the hands of Benito Mussolini's Fascists in November 1926 in an attempt to "stop his mind from working."[1] Written in October of that year as a response to Guido Dorso's book *The Southern Revolution* (Gobetti Ed., 1926), this essay represents the culmination of what had been an intense five year period of political and theoretical writings on the part of the Sardinian intellectual (the PCI, Italian Communist Part, is founded is in 1921, and the Fascists' march on Rome takes place in 1922).[2] Held until after Gramsci's trial and eventual imprisonment, the essay was first published in 1930 as "Some Themes Regarding the Southern Question" in the pages of *Lo stato operaio* (The Workers' State), the Italian Communist Party's theoretical journal produced in exile in Paris. Further elisions of the title have brought it down to simply *The Southern Question,* possibly the most recognizable of Gramscian locutions.

Gramsci's essay remains as provocative today as

it was when it was written. During ten years of political imprisonment, Gramsci continued to meditate on subjects and relationships first proposed within the pages of *The Southern Question*. In the *Quaderni del carcere*[3] (*The Prison Notebooks*), written, as the title suggests, in prison, Gramsci elaborated a notable series of observations and commentary on Italian and world issues. Among the varied list of subjects with which he concerned himself were the relationship between the city and the countryside (North/South), the potentially revolutionary alliance between Northern workers and Southern peasants, and the role and position of intellectuals within the narrative spaces provided by the interaction of diverse polities. Testimony to this work's continued importance is Edward Said's observation that "under-read and under-analyzed [*"The Southern Question"*] goes beyond its tactical relevance to Italian politics in 1926. [It is] a prelude to *The Prison Notebooks* in which [Gramsci] gave, as his towering counterpart Lukacs did not, paramount focus to the territorial, spatial, geographical foundations of social life" (*Culture and Imperialism,* 48/49).[4] My own purpose in re-introducing the essay is to emphasize how Gramsci's analysis of social stratifications of Northern and Southern Italy in 1926 is relevant to current discussions about state formation, diasporas, and strategic alliances. Gramsci's works in general, and *The Southern Question* in particular, have been relevant to Liberation Theology movements from Central and South America to the Indian sub-continent, to the Zapatista movement in Chiapas, and to the continuing debate between the Italian North and South. For Italy, the terms of this debate are now, in part, defining its role within the European Union.

Gramsci's discourse on the South had its formal beginnings in "Workers and Peasants," an article (also translated herein) published in *L'Ordine Nuovo* in 1920 and referred to in the pages of *The Southern Question*.[5] This citation serves to establish the stance of the Turin Communists regarding the Southern Question, and provides a summary outline of the alliances that must be in place in order to "promote peace between the city and the countryside, between the North and the South" (76). It was with such proposals that Gramsci broke with the "southernist" tradition that prevailed among Southern intellectuals. Many "southernists" were members of the Socialist Party whose view of Italian unity was limited to the exploitability of the nation's resources for the benefit of the bourgeoisie (46-50). Most importantly, however, within the pages of *The Southern Question* Gramsci exposed the racist views vis-à-vis the South that reformist Socialists had helped diffuse:

The South is the ball and chain that prevents a more rapid progress in the civil development of Italy; Southerners are biologically inferior beings, either semi-barbarians, or full out barbarians, by natural destiny . . . The Socialist Party was in great part the vehicle of this bourgeois ideology among the Northern proletariat; the Socialist Party gave its blessing to all the "southernist" literature of the clique of writers of the so-called positivist school, such as Ferri, Sergi, Niceforo, Orano, and their lesser followers, who in articles, in sketches, in stories, in novels, in books of impressions and memoirs, repeated the same tune in different form (37).

The discrepant and contradictory relationship of "southernists" to the Southern masses is representative of what Gramsci described as "a great social disintegration"(55). Within that optic he emphasized the need for an analysis of social stratification as it functioned within Southern society:

Southern society is a large agrarian bloc, made up of three social strata: the large peasant mass, amorphous and disintegrated; the intellectuals of the petty and medium rural bourgeoisie; and the large landowners and great intellectuals. Southern peasants are in perpetual ferment, but as a mass they are unable to give a centralized expression to their aspirations and needs. The middle strata of intellectuals receives the impulses for its political and ideological activity from the peasant base. In the last stage of analysis, the large landlords in the political field, and the great intellectuals in the ideological field, centralize and dominate the whole complex of manifestations (56).

The Southern peasants' relationship to the landlords is described as being mediated by the intellectuals, who originated within the rural bourgeoisie; their role being to centralize and dominate both political and ideological trends. Such a relationship facilitated the creation of "a monstrous agrarian bloc which functions wholly as intermediary and overseer for Northern capitalism and the large banks. Its only goal is to preserve the status quo"(55-60). The historical objective of the proletariat, on the other hand, is to destroy the agrarian bloc by forming a revolutionary alliance between Northern workers and Southern peasants (34).

Gramsci's analysis of North/South relations involves the history of Italian unification, the first phase of which took place in 1860 with Garibaldi's "liberation" of Sicily and the South from Bourbon rule. It soon became obvious to the Southern masses that the effort was to benefit them much less than they had been led to believe. The collaboration of Northern "liberators" with Southern landowners further rooted the imbalances that had existed under the Bourbons. Rebellion against the "liberating" troops was branded as criminal (*brigantaggio*) and was strongly repressed, with the engagement of more than half of the young national armed forces.

With the failure of unification at its primary stage, Gramsci identified potential alliances for setting the national project on a more equitable track. Two incidents in particular served to illustrate the uneasy state of the Italian nation. The first was the set of events surrounding the 1919 formation and activity of the Young Sardegna Society. This Society was organized in an attempt to form a regional bloc including "all Sardinians on the island and on the mainland [...] capable of exercising useful pressure on the government to maintain the promises made to the soldiers during the war"(40). However, the regional alliance was undermined by the proposal made by the attending group of Sardinian Communists, who presented options for an alliance either with "the gentry of Sardegna – the local overseers of capitalist exploitation [or] with the workers of the mainland, who were for the abolition of exploitation and emancipation of the oppressed"(42). Sardinian workers sided with the latter, denying the regional bloc and embarking on the more treacherous road of an inter-regional workers alliance.

The second event that offered the occasion for optimism regarding development of alliances between groups with similar interests was that of the

Sassari Brigade. The Brigade was made up of Sardinian soldiers who were sent into Turin in August of 1917 to quell a workers' insurrection. While the Brigade was welcomed by "ladies and gentlemen who offered the soldiers flowers, cigars and fruit"(43), the soldiers, coming in contact with the protesting Sardinian workers, underwent a change of heart and became educated as to the conditions of the workers and the situation. Such was the effect of the workers on the Brigade that "on the eve of the general strike of July 20-21, the Brigade was removed from Turin, the older soldiers were discharged, and the unit was split into three"(44).

In fact, these incidents illustrate the struggle for power as it took place between the Moderates and the Liberal Democrats in the process of unifying Italy. The latter, represented by the Action Party of Giuseppe Mazzini and Giuseppe Garibaldi, failed to formulate a program in answer to the needs of the popular masses, in particular the peasantry, just as the Sardinian Action Party (or Young Sardegna) had failed to support the workers and peasants in the first anecdote recounted. The victory of the Moderates, under the leadership of Count Cavour, was achieved by gaining the collaboration of intellectuals and the bourgeoisie, both of whom came to dictate the choices that determined the direction in which both state and society developed post-unification. Within this context, the Southern Question could no longer merely be viewed as the history of Southern backwardness, but was expanded to implicate the choices made by the ruling class regarding particular interests in the development of the nation. Thus, Gramsci's view that the Southern Question was a product of capitalism that could only be resolvable only through socialist revolution, marked a departure from the traditional "southernist" view.

Of course, the alliance proposed by Gramsci and the Torino Communists in *L'Ordine Nuovo* (32-33) did not take place. This was mostly due to the already stated prejudice that "the South represented a "lead-ball" for Italy, and that the modern and industrial northern civilization would have fared better without this "lead-ball" dragging it down" (*Il Risorgimento*, 80-81).[6] Instead of an alliance, the industrial development of the country resulted in an inversion by which Southerners emigrated North, thus providing the direly needed labor force for northern industries. This short-circuit, along with the massive emigration outside of Italy that preceded and continued alongside the internal migration, seemed to negate the possibility of the kind of development Gramsci had imagined. Even as southern workers in the North resisted exploitation by taking active part in the great protests and industrial rebellions of the 1960s and 1970s, thereby providing a commonality between the two poles of northern and southern workers within the labor force, the alliance remained incomplete.[7]

Today's Southern Question, though no longer easily classifiable by the parameters of city/country-side or peasant/industrial worker, nevertheless persists in the conditions that influence civil life, "meaning, the state of public services and administration, the political system" (Bevilacqua, 122).[8] Now, almost eighty years after the composition of *The Southern Question,* many of the problematics regarding the relationship of the South to the North remain unresolved. The terms of the equation, over the last decade or so, have been complicated by a number of factors, among which is Italy's transformation from a country of emigration to a country of immigration.

In a 1971 speech on the Southern Question, in the city of Palermo, Enrico Berlinguer, then secretary of the PCI, related how "the degradation of the South consists not in [its being] forgotten, but in [its being] utilized so as to guarantee and exalt the economic development of the nation."[9] Berlinguer also noted an interesting appropriation of Gramsci's exhortation to Northern workers to unite with Southern peasants by La Malfa, then secretary of the PRI (Italian Republican party). La Malfa had extended an invitation "to the workers of the North to show solidarity with Southern populations" (4). His suggestion, while appearing to mirror Gramsci's call for an alliance, merely implied that Northern workers could, by tightening their belts, allow corporations and industries to increase their earnings, which, in turn, would provide capital for investment in the South. Such a proposal does not work for the interests of either Northern or Southern populations – by orienting "industrial production to useful work that will promote peace between the city and the countryside, between North and South"(3). It is for the benefit of industries and corporations, and reflects a modern-day "southernist" stance.

The degradation of Southerners persists in the political discourse of such groups as the *Lega Nord* (the Northern League), an autonomist/separatist party, much of whose rhetoric is based on positivist constructions of Northern racial superiority and Southern inferiority.[10] According to some commentators, the success of the Lega in the elections of June 1993 was indicative of the fact that Northern hegemony over the South had not really changed since unification.[11] It might appear that, within the rhetoric of federalism, Lega's Umberto Bossi's expressions regarding the North/South relationship preserve the misconceptions of a majority of Northern populations regarding the South. By injecting his view of history with a hint of altruism, Bossi spews his prejudices in statements such as:

We are tired of being a land of invasion, first from the South and now from the Third World. There is no work, and opening our doors to immigrants to then leave them in miserable conditions is a crime (36).[12]

And:

In these less than disastrous conditions, we witness day after day the conflict between an Italy that aspires to become European with its head held high, creating a modern nation, democratic and civil, and the forces that orbit around the public machinery and are fed by it, the forces whose objectives are to become part of the African peninsula (53).

Today, though having unsuccessfully tried to tone down its rhetoric, the Lega in all its Northern manifestations is well represented in politics and a force to be dealt with. Berlusconi's Forza Italia has chosen to ally itself with the divisive forces of the Lega and Alleanza Nazionale (the contemporary manifestation of the Italian Fascist party) in its rabid cold-war anti-Communist style government. With the increase in immigration the North has grown more and more xenophobic, and the presence of markedly different populations has made the xenophobia that much more explicit. In an incident in late 2000, a group of Lega supporters invaded a plot of land that had been set apart by the government to enable a Muslim community to construct a mosque. These individuals showed their disdain for the beliefs of Islam and their disrespect and their hate of those who they conceive as irreconcilably different, by bringing hogs to urinate and defecate on the apportioned land. Such events call for a reconsideration of Gramscian writings, and their application to a contemporary context that requires a revisioning and a redrawing of alliances, either nationally or toward an extra-national sphere.

The events of 1994 represent a crux of convergence for the issues addressed by Antonio Gramsci in the pages of *The Southern Question*. The results of the 1994 elections, in which a right-wing alliance came to power, further emphasize the North/South division and the exertion of Northern hegemony. The victorious alliance between the then newly-formed Forza Italia, representative of Northern industrialism, the neo-fascist MSI (Movimento Sociale Italiano), reborn as Alleanza Nazionale (National Alliance), and the Lega Lombarda defeated a Left that, although fragmented, not only held its ground but actually gained in the Southern regions. These developments parallel the situation at the time when Gramsci found it necessary to address the issues contained in the pages of *The Southern Question*. The contemporary triumvirate, while having quickly failed due to internal discord, was as ominous an alliance as the one formed in the early twenties which allowed the rise of Fascism. The search for national stability by turning emphatically to the right, pointed to issues that indicated a certain parallelism between Italian unification and European unity.

After years of governmental stability under the leadership of Romano Prodi's PDS, followed by a progression of insipid center-left politics under Massimo D'Alema, the Right regrouped and once again gained ground through the regional elections of 2000. Newspaper headlines on the day following the elections of April 16, 2000, blared *Tutto il Nord al Polo e Lega* ("The North Goes to the League and Pole,"*La Repubblica*). Forza Italia, the Lega Nord and Alleanza Nazionale once again formed an alliance ready to declaim victory. Berlusconi, leader of Forza Italia, and his allies have instituted a politics of extremes in which their main electoral platform has been "freedom." Wholly dismissing the historical record, and the fact that Christian Democrats and a variety of center-right coalitions had kept the Italian Communist Party out of government since 1948, Berlusconi has succeeded in painting for his followers an Italy that is some sort of Gulag in which Communists had been suppressing the democratic freedoms of Italians for the past fifty years.

Berlusconi's rhetoric and the foundation of *"La casa della libertà"* (The House of Freedom), an imaginary site in which to house and protect the freedoms supposedly under threat, may sound ludicrous but they had their effect. And yet, these elections served once more to consolidate a view of Italy that is useful in its unfortunate repetition. The spring 2000 Regional elections made the divisions clear. While in 1994 the gains of the Left in the South might have been veiled by the size and specificity of some of the parties, in the 2000 elections they could not have been more evident. The Left that gained support in the South was not the old internationalist PCI, but rather a Left-party rooted in the local as its point of departure.

The most notable of these cases was that of Mayor Giovanni Bassolino of Naples. Elected with a clear and large majority in 1994, his mandate as mayor of the problematic city was renewed by re-election with 73% of the vote in 1999. In the spring 2000 elections, Bassolino brought to the Campania Region a similarly strong politics with a decisive victory as Regional President. Bassolino's book, *La repubblica delle città* (*The Republic of Cities*; Rome: Donzelli, 1996), outlines concepts that he brought to bear as Mayor of Naples in the transformation of that city. His example goes hand in hand with a number of other positive results in the renovation of the South's self-image, civic and social life. Among the important publications that have joined the dialogue lately are Mario Alcaro's *Sull'identità merdionale:*

Forme di una cultura mediterranea (*On Southern Identity: Forms of a Mediterranean Culture*), Franco Cassano's *Il pensiero meridiano* (*Meridian Thought*), and Franco Piperno's *Elogio dello spirito pubblico meridionale: genius loci e individuo sociale* (*In Praise of the Southern Public Spirit: Genius loci and Social Individual*). The overall consensus among contemporary intellectuals is that the Southern Question must be considered not in terms of Northern development but on its own terms. These publications and their authors engage not in qualitative comparisons but in assessing the viability of Southern elements that may lead to the application of new terms of development based on alternative values.

Nevertheless, the stark divisions illuminated by the 2000 elections were emphasized by the apparent xenophobia that took the upper hand in the 2001 national elections. The re-emergence of the Berlusconi-Bossi-Fini triumvirate represents an unfortunate turn for the case not only of Italian unity, but for European unity as well. Hedging on its own convictions, the North plays a game of chicken on the moral ground of immigration issues as long as it keeps one eye shut toward Italy's own emigrant history. The right has chosen to revisit this history in the form of giving the vote to Italians abroad. The Center-right views this generally unknown mass of "foreign Italians" as their constituents. Until recently, this is also how the South was regarded. Having taken for granted one group and lost a large portion of it, the Center-right is making similar assumptions vis-à-vis emigrated Italians, counting their votes before they are cast. Historically, no attempt has ever been made to know the emigrated reality. Assumptions about its political character are made that may or may not meet expectations. In the case of this newly devised contingent, its true political nature remains to be seen. However, what is most painfully obvious is that, once again the same people are being tapped as a token resource to maintain a political and social system that has failed them and their kin repeatedly.

The capper to all this is that, blinded by Berlusconi's ultra bright smile, Italian American officialdom has chosen to bathe in the cynical light of the only Italian government that has recognized the presence of the dispersed children of the motherland since Mussolini. In May 2004, the Sons of Italy, the largest Italian American organization, presented Prime Minister Silvio Berlusconi with its Man of Courage Award for having supported U.S. intervention in Iraq.

The Southern Question Beyond Italy

To truly appreciate the breadth and import of *The Southern Question*, I believe that another inextricable, yet neglected, component of the Southern Question must be addressed. I am referring to the Southern Italian emigrant diaspora. Given the extensive emigration from the South to foreign lands, I believe that it is possible to recuperate various aspects of Gramsci's critique of the Italian nation-state by viewing emigrants as a decontextualized expression of the contradictory process of Italian state formation.[13] The inclusion of those externalized historics into the equation of both country of origin and receptor country enables us to rethink concepts of nation, race and ethnicity, their role in the construction of Italian unification and their influence on international relations.

Individuals of various Italian expatriate generations are renewing contact with their cultural background, which necessitates a critical encounter with the history of Italian emigration on terms that have never before been approached; that is, from the perspective of the e/im-migrants themselves. Only as that decontextualized component of the South grows in its awareness of its background and history, and with a re-assessment of the national conditions that engendered emigration, can a fully operable critique of the Italian nation and all its myths truly be undertaken.

The elaboration and historicization of the Italian immigrant experience will invariably bring to light the commonalities that tie Italians to minority and immigrant groups that are marginal to the official power structure of various nations. While over the decades the history that Italian immigrants have shared with other ethnic and minority groups in North America has been greatly voided by pressures to assimilate to dominant cultural norms, a potential realignment with non-dominant (subaltern) groups may still be possible. As a Southern Italian e/immigrant, I offer this new translation of *The Southern Question* in the spirit of alliance with groups that are today living the history that the Italian immigrant community seems to have long denied. I also offer it up to Italian immigrants in all parts of the globe as a path through which to revive and acknowledge a neglected history. Finally, that I can now translate this critical piece of writing by one of the South's great intellectuals represents in itself a coming to full circle for the importance of the piece and the maturation of certain attitudes and historical perspectives within Italian immigrant communities.

While *The Southern Question* deals particularly with the North/South relationship in Italy, its usefulness as a tool of analysis should not be limited to the Italian context. Antonio Gramsci's concerns were to promote a "national popular" culture which would reflect the peculiarities of Italian cultural diversity and to enable different social strata in the North and South to form new alliances, ones that would defy the cultural hegemony consolidated at the time of national unification.[14] In addition, Gramsci's concept of new alliances has been influential for a number of movements and intellectuals, such as those associated with the Birmingham Cultural Studies Collective. Stuart Hall, in his "Gramsci's Relevance for the Study of Race and Ethnicity," as elsewhere, offers useful examples of Gramscian application to contemporary situations concerning issues of race, ethnicity, and colonialism.[15] Renate Holub, in her *Antonio Gramsci: Beyond Marxism and Postmodernism* (Routledge, 1992), outlines lines of resistance made available to feminist thought through Gramscian elaborations. Lucia Chiavola Birnbaum has analyzed sites of resistance to cultural officialdom through long-standing popular rituals and "spiritual" representations in *Black Madonnas: Feminism, Religion and Politics in Italy* (Northeastern University Press, 1993). And Cornell West, Gramscian by self-definition is adamant on the importance of Gramsci's concepts for African Americans, and as aids in a transition toward inclusive and collaborative politics and human relations.

These applications do not mean to suggest a simple overlaying of Gramscian ideas on separately evolved historical situations. Rather, merely that one view of the national struggle as it is carried out by non-dominant groups within the boundaries of a single nation may illuminate parallel patterns in varying situations. It is only logical that the Gramscian concept of new alliances should become relevant now to Italian Americans who, as they slowly acknowledge their historically dysfunctional relationship to so-called "white" America, are following the lead of Latino and Latinas, Asian and African Americans and others in their reflections on cultural specificity.

The circumstances that condition the relationship between industrial and non-industrial societies, or First and Third-World societies, as well as the inequities extant between populations within the First-World, are consistently comparable, even in their differences, with the North/South relationship in Italy. Much as they functioned, and to some extent continue to function, in the North/South binarism, oppositions such as First World/Third World, Black/White, etc. are similarly limited in scope because they are based upon, and therefore tend to validate conditions predicated by the backwardness of one of the elements vis-à-vis the superiority of the other. Gramsci's relevance resides in the concrete possibilities opened by his theories; always breaking down bipolar representations of the North/South relation into a more complex view of social stratification; Gramsci provides more constructive designations that unveil new and pertinent grounds for activist strategies and alliances.

Pasquale Verdicchio,
San Diego

The Southern Question

Some Aspects of the Southern Question

The impetus for these notes was provided by the publication of an article on the *Southern Question* in the September 18th issue of *Quarto Stato* under the byline Ulenspiegel,[1] that the directors prefaced with a comical editorial note.[2] Ulenspiegel informs his readers of Guido Dorso's recent book *La rivoluzione meridionale* (Torino: Gobetti Ed., 1925) and alludes to Dorso's assessment of our Party's position on the Southern Question.[3] In their introduction, the editors of *Quarto Stato,* who proclaim themselves to be "young people who have perfect knowledge of the Southern question in its general lines [sic]," offer a collective protest at the idea that the Party can be accorded any merit regarding the issue. Nothing wrong so far; young people of the *Quarto Stato* type have always and everywhere expressed their opinions and protests on paper without causing the paper to rebel. But then these young people add the following: "We have not forgotten that the magic formula of the Turin Communists was: divide the estates among the rural proletariat. That formula is at the antipodes of any sane and realistic vision of the *Southern Question*." At this point it is necessary to set things straight, since of "magic" there is only the impudence and superficial dilettantism of the "young" writers of the *Quarto Stato*.

The "magic formula" was pure invention. The "young" writers of *Quarto Stato* must indeed have a truly low opinion of their extremely intellectual readers, if they dare to so blatantly distort the truth. In fact, here is a passage from *L'Ordine Nuovo* of January 3rd, 1920, which sums up the viewpoint of the Turin Communists[4]:

> The Northern bourgeoisie has subjugated the South of Italy and the Islands, and reduced them to exploitable colonies; by emancipating itself from capitalist slavery, the Northern proletariat will emancipate the Southern peasant masses enslaved to the banks and the parasitic industrialism of the North. The economic and political regeneration of the peasants should not be sought in the division of uncultivated or poorly cultivated lands, but in the solidarity of the industrial proletariat who need, in turn, the solidarity of the peasantry. They have an interest in keeping capitalism from being reborn economically from landed property; and ensuring that Southern Italy and the Islands do not become a military base for capitalist counter-revolution. By imposing workers' control over industry, the proletariat will reorient industry

28

to the production of agricultural machinery for the peasants, clothing and footwear for the peasants, electrical energy for the peasants; they will prevent industry and banks from exploiting the peasants and subjecting them as slaves to the vaults. By breaking autocracy in the factories, by breaking the oppressive apparatus of the capitalist State and installing a workers' State that will subject the capitalists to the law of useful labor, the workers will break all the chains that hold the peasants to their poverty and desperation. By installing a workers' dictatorship, by taking hold of the industries and banks, the proletariat will turn the enormous power of the state apparatus to the aid of the peasants in their struggle against the landowners, against the elements, against misery. The proletariat will provide peasants with credit, set up cooperatives, guarantee security of person and property against looters and carry out public works of reclamation and irrigation. It will do all this because it is in its interest to increase agricultural production, because it is in its interest to have and conserve the solidarity of the peasant masses, because it is in its interest to orient industrial production to useful work that will promote peace between the city and the countryside, between North and South.[5]

This was written in January 1920. Seven years have gone by and we are also seven years older politically; some concepts could be expressed a little better today; one could, and should, better distinguish between the period immediately following the conquest of the

State, characterized simply by workers' control of industry, from successive periods. But what is important here is to note that the fundamental concept of the Turin Communists was not the "magic formula" of land allotment, but that of the political alliance between the Northern workers and the Southern peasants to oust the bourgeoisie from State power. Furthermore, the Turin Communists themselves (though they supported land division as a secondary action to class solidarity) warned against the "miraculous" illusions of mechanically dividing the large estates. In the same article of January 3, 1920, we find: "What can a poor peasant achieve by occupying uncultivated or poorly cultivated lands? Without machinery, without accommodation at the place of work, without credit to tide him over till harvest, without cooperative institutions to purchase the harvest (if the peasant hasn't hung himself from the strongest bush or the least sickly fig tree on his uncultivated land long before harvest time) and save him from the clutches of the usurers, what can a poor peasant achieve by occupation?" And still, we were for the very realistic and not at all "magic" formula of allotting land to the peasants; but we wanted to incorporate this formula into a general revolutionary action of the two classes in alliance, under the direction of the industrial proletariat. The writers of *Quarto Stato* invented the "magic formula" out of the whole cloth and attributed to the Turin Communists, thus demonstrating lack of journalistic seriousness and a lack of scruples reminiscent of drugstore intellectuals. These attitudes too are indicative of political elements that bear significant weight and carry their own consequences.

In the proletarian camp, the Turin Communists have had one undeniable "merit": that of bringing the Southern question to the attention of the workers' vanguard, and identifying it as one of the essential problems of the national politics of the revolutionary proletariat. In this sense they have contributed in practice by lifting the Southern question out of its indistinct, intellectualistic, so-called "concretist" phase, and enabled it to enter a new phase.[6] The revolutionary worker of Turin and Milan became the protagonist of the Southern question in place of the likes of Giustino Fortunato, Gaetano Salvemini, Eugenio Azimonti and Arturo Labriola, to make mention only the great saints dear to the "young" writers of *Quarto Stato*.[7]

The Turin Communists had concretely posed themselves the question of "proletarian hegemony," in other words of the social base of the proletarian dictatorship and of the workers' State. The proletariat can become the leading and dominant class in the measure in which it succeeds in creating a system of class alliances that will permit it to mobilize the

31

majority of the working population against capitalism and the bourgeois State. This means that, in the real class relations as they exist in Italy, the proletariat, in the measure in which it is to be successful, needs to obtain the consensus of the large peasant masses. But the peasant question in Italy is historically determined, it is not the "peasant and agrarian question in general." In Italy the peasant question has, given its specific Italian tradition, for the historical specifics of Italian history, assumed two particularly typical and peculiar forms, the Southern question and the Vatican question. In order to conquer the majority of the peasant masses therefore means that the Italian proletariat must make these two questions its own from a point of view of social life; it must understand the class demands that they represent, and it must incorporate these demands into its revolutionary program of transition. It must place these demands among the objectives for which it struggles.

The first problem to be resolved by the Turin Communists was to modify the political direction and the general ideology of the proletariat itself as a national element that lives within the complex of State life and is subjected, unconsciously, to the influences of the educational system, of newspapers, of bourgeois tradition. It is well known what kind of ideology has been disseminated in innumerable ways by the propagandists of the bourgeoisie among the masses of the North: the South is the ball and chain that prevents a more rapid progress in the civil development of Italy [8]; Southerners are biologically inferior beings, either semi-barbarians or out and out barbarians by natural destiny; if the South is underdeveloped it is not the fault of the capitalist system, or any other historical cause, but of the nature that has made Southerners lazy, incapable, criminal and barbaric. This harsh fate has been only slightly tempered by the purely individual explosion of a few great geniuses, like isolated palms in an arid and sterile desert. The Socialist Party was in great part the vehicle of this bourgeois ideology among the Northern proletariat; the Socialist Party gave its blessing to all the "southernist" literature of the clique of writers of the so-called positivist school, such as Ferri, Sergi, Niceforo, Orano, and their lesser followers, who in articles, sketches, stories, novels, and books of impressions and memoirs, repeated the same tune in different form. [9] Once again "science" was used to crush the wretched and abused, but this time it was dressed in the colours of Socialism, which claimed to be the science of the proletariat.

The Turin Communists reacted energetically against this ideology precisely in Turin itself, where the stories and descriptions of the veterans of the war against "brigands" in the South and the Islands had largely influenced popular tradition and beliefs.[10] They reacted energetically, in practical ways, and were successful in obtaining concrete results of great historical relevance, obtaining in Turin the embryonic forms of the solution to the Southern question.[11]

Moreover, already before the war, an episode occurred in Turin which potentially contained all the action and propaganda carried out by the Communists after the war. When, in 1914, with the death of Pilade Gay, the city's fourth borough was left unattended and the problem of a new candidate arose, a group of the Socialist Section, among whom were the future editors of the *Quarto Stato,* proposed the candidacy of Gaetano Salvemini. At that time Salvemini was the most progressive exponent, in a radical sense, of the peasant masses of the South. He was outside of the Socialist Party, and in fact was leading a vivacious and dangerous campaign against the Socialist Party – this because his affirmations and accusations became, among the Southern working masses, a cause of hate not only toward Turati, Treves, D'Aragona but against the industrial proletariat as a whole.[12] (Many of the bullets that the royal guards fired in 1919, 1920, 1921, and 1922 against the workers were cast from the same lead that served to print Salvemini's articles.) Nevertheless, the Turin group had to take a stand on Salvemini's name; it was explained to Salvemini himself by comrade Ottavio Pastore, who had gone to Florence to obtain an agreement to the candidature:

> The Turin workers want to elect a deputy for the peasants of Puglia. The workers of Turin know that in the general elections of 1913, the peasants of Molfetta and Bitonto were, in the great majority, in favor of Salvemini: administrative pressure by the Giolitti government and the violence of the police and hired thugs prevented the peasants of Puglia from expressing their choice. The workers of Turin do not ask Salvemini for any such guarantees: neither from the Party, nor from a program, nor for discipline to the parliamentary group. Once elected, Salvemini will be accountable to the peasants of Puglia, not to the workers of Turin, who will carry out the electoral propaganda on their own terms and will in no way be indebted by Salvemini's political activity.

Salvemini declined to accept the candidacy, although he was shaken and even moved by the proposal (in those days no one yet spoke of Communist "perfidy," and manners were honorable and unconstrained). He proposed Mussolini as candidate and promised to come to Turin to support the Socialist Party in its electoral struggle.[13] In fact, he held two large meetings at the Chamber of Labor and in Piazza Statuto, amidst the enthusiasm of the masses who viewed and applauded him as the representative of the Southern peasants, oppressed and exploited in more odious and bestial ways that the Northern proletariat.

The approach that this episode potentially contained, but which was intentionally not developed further by Salvemini, was taken up again and applied by the Communists in the period following the war. Let us recall the most significant and symptomatic facts.

In 1919 the Giovane Sardegna (Young Sardegna) society was formed, marking the emergence and premise to what would later be the Partito Sardo d'Azione (Sardinian Action Party).[14] Giovane Sardegna had proposed to unite all Sardinians on the island and on the mainland in a regional bloc, capable of exercising useful pressure on the government to maintain the promises made to the soldiers during the war. The organizer of Giovane Sardegna on the mainland was a certain professor Pietro Nurra, a socialist, who most is today most likely a member of the "young" group which every week discovers in *Quarto Stato* a new horizon to explore. The society was joined by lawyers, professors, and functionaries with the enthusiasm of those who are eager to earn new crosses, commendations, and medals. The constituent assembly, held in Turin for Sardinians living in the Piemonte, was impressive for the sheer numbers in attendance and the number of speakers. The majority in attendance was made up of humble citizens, folks with no discernible qualifications: unskilled laborers, retirees on pensions, former *carabinieri,* former prison guards, former frontier guards who were now managing a wide variety of petty commercial ventures. Everyone was excited at the thought of finding themselves among fellow Sardinians, of hearing speeches about their land, to which they continued to be tied by an innumerable series of family relations, friends, memories, sufferings, and hopes: the hope of returning to their land, but to a more prosperous and rich land that could offer them conditions for living, even if modestly.

The Sardinian Communists, who numbered exactly eight, went to the meeting, presented their motion to the Chair, and requested the opportunity to make a counter-presentation. After the official speaker's fiery and rhetorical presentation, embellished by all the Venuses and Cupids of regionalist oratory; after the participants had cried at the memories of pain suffered and blood spilled in war by Sardinian regiments, and were filled with enthusiasm to the point of delirium with the idea of a united bloc of all the generous sons of Sardegna, it became very difficult to contextualize the counterpresentation.[15] The most optimistic forecasts were, if not for a lynching, then at least for a stroll to the police, after being saved from the "righteous indignation of the crowd." Even so, even though the counterpresentation provoked stupefaction, it was heard with attention and, once the spell was broken, things progressed rapidly and methodically toward the revolutionary conclusion. The dilemma: Are you, poor Sardinian devils, are you for a bloc with the gentry of Sardegna, who have ruined you and are the local overseers of capitalist exploitation? Or are you for a bloc with the revolutionary workers of the mainland, who stand for the abolition of exploitation and emancipation of all who are oppressed? This dilemma was rammed into the heads of those present. The vote was a tremendous success: on one side, a handful of handsomely dressed ladies, functionaries in top-hats, professionals livid with rage and fear, and forty-odd policemen around them to garnish the consensus; on the other side, the multitude of poor devils and women dressed in their party-best, gathered around the tiny Communist cell. An hour later, at the Chamber of Labor, the Sardinian Socialist Education Circle was formed with 256 members. The formation of Giovane Sardegna was postponed *sine die*, and in fact never took place.

This was the political basis for the activity carried out among the soldiers of the *Brigata Sassari,* a brigade with an almost totally regional composition. The Sassari Brigade had taken part in the repression of the insurrectional movement in Turin in August 1917.[16] It was believed that the Brigade, due to the memories of hate that every repressive action leaves in both the masses and in the ranks of the soldiers, would never fraternize with the workers. The Brigade was welcomed by a crowd of ladies and gentlemen who offered the soldiers flowers, cigars and fruit. The soldiers' state of mind is well characterized by this reminiscence of a tannery worker from Sassari involved in the first propaganda polls: "I approached a bivouac of Square X (in the first days the Sardinian soldiers bivouacked in the square as if in a conquered city) and I spoke with a young peasant who had greeted me politely because I was from Sassari, as he was. 'Why have you come to Turin?' 'We have come to shoot the gentry who are on strike.' 'But it is not the gentry who are on strike, it is the workers and they are poor.' 'Here everyone is of the gentry; they wear collars and ties; they earn 30 lire a day; I know poor people, I know how they dress; in Sassari, there we have a lot of poor people; all us peasants, we are poor and earn 1.5 lire a day.' 'But I'm a worker too, and I am poor.' 'You're poor because you're Sardinian.' 'But if I strike with the others will you shoot me too?' The soldier thought for a minute, then placing his hand on my shoulder he said: 'Listen, when you strike with the others, stay home!'"

That was the attitude of large part of the Brigade, which contained only a small number of mine workers from Iglesias. And yet, within a few months, on the eve of the general strike of July 20-21, the Brigade was moved away from Turin, the older soldiers were discharged and the unit was split into three: one third was sent to Aosta, one third to Trieste, and a third to Rome. The Brigade was sent off at night, suddenly; there was no elegant crowd to wish the farewell; their songs, though still songs of war, no longer had the same content as the ones they had sung on arrival.

Did these events pass without consequence? No, they had results that still linger today and continue to function in the depths of the popular masses. These events shed light for a moment on the minds of those who had never thought in that direction and that have since been deeply affected and radically modified. Our archives have been scattered; many documents we ourselves destroyed so as not to provoke arrests and persecutions. But we remember dozens, even hundreds of letters sent from Sardegna to the editorial desk of the *Avanti!* in Turin[17]; letters written by groups, often signed by all the ex-fighters of the Sassari Brigade from a particular town. In uncontrolled and uncontrollable ways, the political attitudes we supported were becoming more diffused; the formation of the Sardinian Action Party was strongly influenced at its base, and it would be possible to recall in this respect episodes that are rich in content and significance.[18]

The last verifiable repercussion of this action

occurred in 1922, when, with the same aim as in the case of the Sassari Brigade, 300 *carabinieri* of the Cagliari Legion were sent to Turin. We, the editors of *Ordine Nuovo,* received a declaration of principle, signed by a large portion of these *carabinieri;* it echoed in every way our position on the Southern problem, and was the decisive proof of the correctness of our approach.

The proletariat had to adopt this approach itself for it to become politically effective: that goes without saying. No mass action is possible if the mass itself is not convinced of the ends they wish to attain and the methods to be applied. The proletariat, in order to be able to govern as a class, has to shed every residue of corporatism, every syndicalist prejudice or incrusta-tion. What does this mean? That, in addition to over-coming distinctions that exist between one trade and another, it is necessary, in order to win the trust and consensus of the peasants and of some semi-proletar-ian categories within the cities, to overcome certain prejudices and conquer certain forms of egoism which can and do subsist within the working class as such, even when craft particularism has vanished. The metal worker, the carpenter, the builder, etc., must not only think as proletarians and no longer as metal worker, carpenter, builder, etc., but they have to take one more step forward: they have to think like workers who are members of a class that aims to lead the peasants and intellectuals. They have to think like a class which can win and build socialism only if it is helped and followed by the large majority of these social strata. If this is not achieved, the proletariat does not become the leading class, and these strata that, in Italy represent the majority of the population, remain under bourgeois leadership enable the State to resist the proletarian assault and wear it down.

Well, what has occurred on the terrain of the Southern question shows that the proletariat has understood its duties. Two events should be kept well in mind: one took place in Turin, the other in Reggio Emilia, in other words the citadel of reformism, class corporatism and working class protectionism cited as an example by "southernists" in their propaganda among the peasants of the South.

After the occupation of the factories, the board of directors of Fiat proposed to the workers that they run the firm as a cooperative. Naturally, the reformists were in favor. And as industrial crisis was looming, the specter of unemployment worried the workers' families. If Fiat were to become a cooperative, a certain job security would be gained by the skilled workers, and especially by the more politically active workers, who were convinced that they were marked for dismissal.

The Socialist Section, led by the communists,

energetically intervened in the question. The workers were told that "a large cooperative firm like Fiat can be taken over by workers, only if the workers have resolved to enter into the system of bourgeois political forces that today govern Italy. The proposition made by the directors of Fiat is part of Giolitti's political plan. What is this plan? The bourgeoisie, even before the war, could no longer govern peacefully. The insurrection of the Sicilian peasants in 1894 and the Milan insurrection of 1898 were the *experimentum crucis* of the Italian bourgeoisie.[19] After the bloody decade of 1890-1900, the bourgeoisie was forced to renounce a dictatorship that was too exclusive, too violent, too direct. It was faced with simultaneous, even if not coordinated, insurrections from both Southern peasants and Northern workers. In the new century, the dominant class inaugurated a new policy of class alliances, of political class blocs, a politics of bourgeois democracy. It had to choose: either a rural democracy – in other words, an alliance with the peasants of the South, a free trade policy of universal suffrage, of administrative decentralization and low prices for industrial products – or a capitalist/worker industrial block, without universal suffrage, with tariff barriers, with the preservation of a highly centralized State (the expression of bourgeois dominion over the peasants, especially in the South and the Islands), and with a reformist policy on wages and trade union freedoms. Not surprisingly, it chose the second solution. Giolitti personified bourgeois rule; the Socialist Party became the instrument of Giolitti's policies. If you look closely, the most radical crises of the socialist and workers' movement take place in the decade 1890-1900. The masses react spontaneously against the policy of the reformist leaders. Syndicalism was born, which is the instinctive, elementary, primitive but healthy expression of working class reaction against the bloc with the bourgeoisie and in support of a bloc with the peasants, *and above all with Southern peasants.*[20] Precisely that: indeed, in a certain sense, syndicalism is a weak attempt on the part of Southern peasants, represented by their most able intellectuals, to lead the proletariat. Who forms the leading nucleus of Italian syndicalism, what is the ideological essence of Italian syndicalism? The leading nucleus of syndicalism is made up almost exclusively of Southerners: Labriola, Leone, Longobardi, Orano. The ideological essence of syndicalism is a new liberalism that is more energetic, more aggressive, and more pugnacious than the traditional variety. If you look closely, there are two fundamental terms around which the successive crises of syndicalism and the gradual passage of syndicalist leaders into the bourgeois camp take place: emigration and free trade, two themes closely tied to Southernism. The phenomenon of emigration gives rise to Enrico Corradini's concept of the "proletarian nation." The Libyan war is taken by a whole layer of intellectuals to be the beginning of the offensive of the "great proletarian" against a capitalist and plutocratic world.[21] A whole group of syndicalists moves over to nationalism, indeed the Nationalist Party is originally founded by ex-syndicalist intellectuals (Monicelli, Forges-Davanzati, Maraviglia). Labriola's book, *Storia di 10 anni* (*A History of Ten Years*) (from 1890 to 1900) is the most typical and characteristic expression of this anti-Giolittian and Southernist neo-liberalism.

In these ten years, capitalism becomes stronger and develops and directs a great part of its activity toward the agriculture of the Po Valley. The most salient events of these ten years are the mass strikes of the agricultural workers of the Po Valley. A profound upheaval takes place among the Northern peasants; a deep class differentiation occurs (the number of landless laborers [*braccianti*] increases by 50%, according to the 1911 census), and there is a corresponding reorganization of political currents and spiritual attitudes. Christian democracy and Mussolinism are the two most outstanding products of the period. Romagna is the regional crucible of these two new activities, as the *bracciante* seem to have become the social protagonist of the political struggle. Social democracy, along with its organs of the left (*Azione* of

Cesena), as well as Mussolinism, quickly fall under the control of the "southernists." *Azione* of Cesena is a regional edition of Gaetano Salvemini's *Unità*. The *Avanti!,* under the direction of Mussolini, slowly but surely transforms itself into a tribune for syndicalist and southernist writers. The likes of Fancello, Lanzillo, Panunzio and Ciccotti become frequent contributors; Salvemini himself does not hide his sympathy for Mussolini, who also becomes the darling of Prezzolini's *Voce*.[22] Everyone remembers that, in actuality, when Mussolini left *Avanti!* and the Socialist Party he was surrounded by this cohort of syndicalists and "southernists."[23]

The most notable result of this period in the revolutionary field is the Red Week of June 1914. The Romagna and the Marche regions are the epicenter of Red Week.[24] In the field of bourgeois politics, the most notable repercussion is the Gentiloni pact. Since the Socialist Party, as a result of the rural movements of the Po Valley, had returned after 1910 to an intransigent tactic, the industrial bloc supported and represented by Giolitti lost its effectiveness; and Giolitti shifted his gun to the other shoulder. He substituted the alliance between the bourgeois and the workers with one between the bourgeois and the Catholics, who represented the peasant masses of Northern and Central Italy. With this alliance, Sonnino's Conservative Party was completely destroyed, a very small cell organized around Antonio Salandra in Southern Italy being the only survivor.[25] The war and the postwar period saw the development of a series of molecular processes of the highest importance within the bourgeois class. Salandra and Nitti were the first two Southern heads of government (not to mention the Sicilians, such as Crispi, who was the most energetic representative of the bourgeois dictatorship in the nineteenth century).[26] They attempted to actualize the industrial bourgeois-Southern landowner plan, Salandra on the conservative side and Nitti on the democratic (both these heads of government were solidly aided by the newspaper *Corriere della Sera,* in other words by the Lombard textile industry). Already, during the war, Salandra attempted to shift, in the favor of the South, the technical forces of the State organization: to substitute the Giolittian State personnel with a new personnel that would embody the new political course of the bourgeoisie. In 1917-18, the newspaper *La Stampa* campaigned for a close collaboration between Giolittians and Socialists in order to prevent the *Apulianization* of the State. The campaign was undertaken in *La Stampa* by Francesco Ciccotti, in other words it is a *de facto* expression of the agreement that existed between Giolitti and the reformists. The question was not a small one, and the Giolittians, in defensive obstinacy, went so far as to surpass the limits allowed a party of the grand bourgeoisie; they went as far as demonstrations of anti-patriotism and defeatism. Today Giolitti is again in power, again the grand bourgeoisie puts its trust in him, as a result of the panic that fills it when faced by the impetuous movement of the popular masses. Giolitti wants to tame the workers of Turin. He has beaten them twice: during the strike of April and in the occupation of the factories, both times with the help of the General Confederation of Labor (CGL), namely corporative reformism. He now claims that he can tie them into the bourgeois State system. What will in fact happen if the skilled workers of Fiat decide to accept the board's proposals? The present industrial shares will become debentures: in other words, the cooperative will have to pay to debenture holders a fixed dividend, whatever the turnover may be. Fiat will be totally isolated from all credit agencies, which will remain in the hands of the bourgeoisie and in whose interest it is to have the workers at their mercy. The skilled workers will necessarily have to bind themselves to the State, which will "come to the aid of the workers" through the activity of the working-class deputies, through the subordination of the workers' political Party to government policies. This is Giolitti's plan in its full application. The Turin proletarians will no longer exist as an independent class, only as an appendage of the bourgeois State. Class corporatism will have triumphed, but the proletariat will have lost its position and its role as leader and guide. It will appear privileged to the mass of poorer workers. To the peasants it will appear as an exploiter just like the bourgeoisie, because the bourgeoisie, as always, will present the privileged nuclei of the working class to the peasant masses as the sole cause of their ills and their misery.

The skilled workers of Fiat almost unanimously accepted this point of view, and the board's proposals were rejected. But this experiment was not sufficient. The Turin proletariat, through a whole series of actions, had shown that it had achieved a very high level of political maturity and capability. The technicians and the white-collar workers in the factories were able to improve their conditions in 1919 only with the backing of the workers. To break the militancy of the technicians, the employers proposed to the workers that they themselves nominate, through elections, new squad and shop foremen. The workers rejected the proposal, even though they had many differences with the technician, who had always been an instrument of repression and persecution for the bosses. At that point, the press waged a rabid campaign in order to isolate the technicians, highlighting their very high salaries, which reached as much as 7,000 lire a month. Skilled workers also gave support to the agitation of the manual laborers, and it was only in this way that the latter succeeded in winning their demands. Within the factories, all privileges and forms of exploitation of the less skilled by the more skilled were done away with. Through these actions the proletarian vanguard earned its social position as avant garde. This was the basis upon which the Communist Path developed in Turin. But outside of Turin? Well, we had expressly wanted to take the problem outside of Turin, and precisely to Reggio Emilia, where there existed the greatest concentration of reformism and class corporatism.[27]

Reggio Emilia had always been a target of the "southernists." A phrase of Camillo Prampolini's, "Italy is made up of Northerners and Sowtherners," was exemplary of the violent hatred that was disseminated among Southerners against the workers of the North.[28] In Reggio Emilia a problem arose similar to the one at Fiat: a large factory was to pass into the hands of the workers as a cooperative. The reformists of Reggio were enthusiastic about the project and trumpeted its praises in their press and at meetings. A Communist from Turin went to Reggio, took the floor at a factory meeting, outlined the entire North/South dispute, and the miracle was achieved. The great majority of the workers rejected the reformist and corporate position. It had been demonstrated that the reformists did not represent the spirit of the Reggio workers; they only represented their passivity and other negative traits. They had succeeded in establishing a political monopoly, due to the notable concentration in their ranks of organizers and propagandists with certain professional talents, and therefore were able to prevent the development and organization of a revolutionary current. But the presence of a capable revolutionary movement had been enough to thwart them and show that the Reggio workers were valiant fighters and not swine raised on government fodder.

In April 1921, 5000 revolutionary workers were fired by Fiat, the Workers' Councils were abolished, real wages were cut. In Reggio Emilia something similar most likely took place. In other words, the workers were defeated. But were their sacrifices meaningless? We do not believe so. Rather, we are certain that they were not meaningless. It is of course difficult to adduce a series of great mass events that prove the immediate and lightning effectiveness of actions. In any case, as far as peasants are concerned, proof is always difficult if not impossible; it is even more difficult in the case of Southern peasant masses.

The South can be defined as a great social disintegration. The peasants, who make up the largest part of the population, have no cohesion among themselves. (Of course, some exceptions are worthy of note: Puglia, Sardegna, Sicilia, where special characteristics exist within the large frame of the Southern structure). Southern society is a large agrarian bloc made up of three social strata: the large peasant mass, amorphous and disintegrated; the intellectuals of the petty and medium rural bourgeoisie; and the large landowners and the great intellectuals. Southern peasants are in perpetual ferment, but as a mass they are unable to give a centralized expression to their aspirations and needs. The middle strata of intellectuals receives the impulses for its political and ideological activity from the peasant base. In the last stage of analysis, the large landlords in the political field and the great intellectuals in the ideological field centralize and dominate the whole complex of manifestations. Naturally, it is in the ideological field that centralization is verified with major efficiency and precision. Giustino Fortunato and Benedetto Croce represent thus the keystones of the Southern system and, in a certain sense, are the two major figures of Italian reaction.[29]

Southern intellectuals are one of the most interesting and important social strata in Italian national life. To convince oneself of this, one has only to think that more than three-fifths of the State bureaucracy is made up of Southerners. Now, to understand the particular psychology of Southern intellectuals, it is necessary to keep in mind certain factual data:

1. In every country, the intellectual strata has been radically altered by the development of capitalism. The old type of intellectual was the organizing element in societies with a mostly peasant and artisan base. To organize the State and to organize commerce the dominant class bred a particular type of intellectual: the technical organizer, the specialist of applied science. In societies where the economic forces have developed in a capitalist direction, to the point where they have absorbed the major part of national activity, it is this second type of intellectual that has prevailed, with all its characteristics of order and intellectual discipline. On the other hand, in countries where agriculture still plays a considerable or even preponderant role, the old type of intellectual still prevails, providing the large part of State personnel. Locally too, in the villages and the small country towns, this intellectual has the function of intermediary between the peasant and the administration in general. In Southern Italy this type predominates, with all its characteristics: democratic in its peasant face, reactionary when facing the big landowners and the government; given to politicking, corruption and disloyalty. The traditional cast of Southern political parties would be impossible to understand, if one did not taken into account the characteristics of this social strata.

2. The Southern intellectual comes mainly from the rural bourgeoisie, a social layer that is still important in the South. This class is made up of the petty and medium landowner who is not a peasant, who does not work the land, who would be ashamed to be a farmer, but who wants to extract a convenient life from the little land that he owns, whether through lease for rent or sharecropping. This social class also desires to send its sons to university or seminary, to provide dowries for its daughters, who must marry officers or civil functionaries of the State. From this social class, the intellectuals derive a fierce antipathy for the working peasants, whom they consider a machine for work that must be bled dry to the bone and that can be easily substituted given the overabundance of the workers' population. They also acquire the atavistic and instinctive fear of the peasant and his destructive violence; therefore their hypocrisy and highly refined art of deception, with which they tame the peasant masses.

3. Since the clergy belongs to the social group of intellectuals, it is necessary to note the features that distinguish the Southern clergy as a whole from the Northern clergy. The Northern priest is generally the son of an artisan or a peasant; he has democratic sentiments and stronger ties to the peasant masses.

Morally, he is more correct than the Southern priest, who often lives more or less openly with a woman. As such, the Northern priest exercises a more complete spiritual function, in that he guides the activity of a family. In the North, the separation of Church and State and the expropriation of ecclesiastical holdings has been more radical than in the South, where parishes and convents, either retained or reconstituted considerable wealth, both as goods and real estate. In the South, the priest represents for the peasant: 1. a land administrator with whom the peasant has to enter into conflict due to the question of rent; 2. a usurer who requires extremely high rates of interest and manipulates religion so as to assure payment of either the rent or interests owed; 3. a man subject to all common passions (women and money), and who therefore inspires no confidence in his discretion and impartiality from a spiritual point of view. Confession therefore exercises only a minimal guiding role, and the Southern peasant, while often superstitious in a pagan sense, is not clerical. All this in its complexity explains why in the South the Popular Party (except in some parts of Sicily) does not have a significant position, and lacks a network of institutions and mass organizations. The peasants' attitude regarding the clergy can be summarized in the popular saying: "A priest is a priest on the altar; outside he is a man like all others."

The Southern peasant is bound to the large landowner through the mediation of the intellectual. The peasant movements, insofar as they do not take, even formally, the form of autonomous and independent mass organizations (in other words, with the ability to select cadres of peasant origin and to register and accumulate the differentiations and progress realized within the movement), always end up by finding their place among the ordinary articulations of the State apparatus – cities, provinces, chamber of deputies. This takes place through the composition and undoing of the local parties, whose personnel is made up of intellectuals, but who are controlled by the large landowners and their agents, like Salandra, Orlando, Di Cesarò.[30] The war seemed to introduce a new element into this type of organizations with the veterans movement, in which the peasant-soldiers and the intellectuals-officers formed a bloc more united amongst themselves and in a certain measure antagonistic toward the large landowners. It did not last long, however it last has residues found in the National Union as conceived by Amendola: it has a sliver of existence thanks to his anti-fascism. But given the lack of any tradition of *explicit* organization among the *democratic* intellectuals of the South, this bloc could change from a fragile hint of water to swollen torrent in a different political climate. The only region where the Veterans' movement achieved a more precise profile, and succeeded in creating a more solid social structure, was Sardegna. And this was understandable: precisely because in Sardegna the class of large landowners is very tenuous, it has no function and does not have the ancient intellectual, cultural and governmental traditions that it does in the continental South. The push from below, exercised by the masses of peasants and shepherds, does not find a suffocating counterweight in the superior social stratum of large landowners. The intellectual leaders take the full force of this pressure and make forward gains more notable than those of the National Union. The Sicilian situation has characteristics that differentiate it strongly from both Sardegna and the South. The large landowners are more cohesive and resolute than they are in the continental South. In addition, there exists a certain amount of industry and a very well developed commercialism (Sicily is the richest region of the South, and one of Italy's richest). The upper classes are very much aware of their importance within national life, and make their weight felt. Sicily and Piedmont are the regions that have given the greatest number of political leaders to the Italian State, the two regions that have exercised a pre-eminent role since 1870. Sicilian popular masses are more advanced than those of the South, but their progress has taken on a typically Sicilian form.

There exists a Sicilian Socialism of the masses that has a peculiar tradition and development; in the 1922 Chamber, approximately twenty of fifty-two deputies were elected on the island.

We have said that the Southern peasant is bound to the large landowners through the mediation of the intellectual. This type of organization is the most common type in the whole of the continental South and in Sicily. It creates a monstrous agrarian bloc which functions wholly as intermediary and overseer for Northern capitalism and the large banks. Its only goal is to preserve the status quo. Within it there shines no intellectual light, exists no program, no drive toward betterment and progress. If any ideas or programs have been put forward, they have had their origin outside of the South, in agrarian-conservative political groups, especially from Tuscany, who in Parliament were associated with the conservatives of the Southern agrarian bloc. Sonnino and Franchetti were among the few intelligent bourgeois who posed the Southern question as a national question, and outlined a government plan for its solution.[31]

What was Sonnino and Franchetti's point of view? That Southern Italy needed to have an independent middle stratum that could function as "public opinion," as it was called then, and that would, on one hand, limit the cruel and arbitrary actions of the landowners and, on the other, moderate the insurrectionism of the poor peasants. Sonnino and Franchetti had been terrified by the popularity that the Bakuninist ideas of the First International had enjoyed in Southern Italy. This fear caused them to commit some blunders that were often grotesque. For example, in one of their publications, reference is made to the fact that a popular tavern or trattoria in a town of Calabria (I am quoting from memory) is called "The Strikers," in order to demonstrate how widespread and deep-rooted internationalist ideas are. If true (and it must be true, given the intellectual probity of the authors), the fact is more simply explained if one recalls that there are numerous Albanian settlements in the South, and that the Albanian word *skipetari* has undergone the strangest and most bizarre distortions in the various dialects (thus, certain documents of the Venetian Republic speak of military formations of *"S'ciopetà"*).[32] It is not so much that Bakunin's ideas were widespread in the South, as that the situation suggested to Bakunin these theories. Certainly the poor Southern peasants were thinking of a great "undoing" (revolt) well before Bakunin's brain had thought out the theory of "pandestruction."

Sonnino and Franchetti's governing plan never even began to be put into practice. And it could not be. The nexus of North and South relations in the organization of the national economy and the State was such that the birth of a broad middle class of an economic nature (meaning then the birth of a broad capitalist bourgeoisie) was made almost impossible. Any accumulation of capital on the spot, and every accumulation of savings was made impossible by the fiscal and customs system; and by the fact that the capitalist owners of companies did not transform their profits into new capital on the spot because they were not from the region. When emigration reached the gigantic proportions that it did in the twentieth century, and the first remittances began to flood in from America, liberal economists cried triumphantly that Sonnino's dream had come true. A silent revolution was said to be taking place in the South, one that slowly but surely would alter the social and economic structure of the country. But the State intervened and the silent revolution was stifled at birth. The government offered treasury bonds with guaranteed interest, and the emigrants and their families were transformed from agents of the silent revolution to agents that would give the State the financial means by which to subsidize the parasitic industries of the North. Francesco Nitti who, on the democratic level was formally external to the Southern agrarian bloc, could have appeared to be an effective realizer of Sonnino's plan, was instead the best agent for Northern capitalism in raking in the last resources of Southern savings. The thousands of millions swallowed up by the *Banca di Sconto* (Savings Bank) were almost all from the South: the 400,000 creditors of the *Banca Italiana di Sconto* were overwhelmingly Southern savers.

Over and above the agrarian bloc, there functions in the South an intellectual bloc that in practice has served, so far, to prevent the cracks in the agrarian bloc from becoming too dangerous and causing a landslide. The major exponents of this intellectual bloc are Giustino Fortunato and Benedetto Croce, who can therefore be considered the most active reactionaries of the whole peninsula.

We have already said that Southern Italy is a great social disintegration. This formula can be applied not only to the peasants, but also to the intellectuals. It is notable that in the South, side by side with immense property holdings there have existed, and continue to exist, great accumulations of culture and intelligence in single individuals, or in small groups of great intellectuals, while no organization of middle culture exists.[33] The South has the Laterza publishing house and the review *La Critica,* and there are Academies and cultural bodies of great erudition; but there are no small- or medium-sized reviews, there are no publishing houses to act as gathering points for the middle layer of Southern intellectuals.[34] The Southerners who have tried to leave the agrarian bloc, and have sought to pose the Southern question in a radical form, have found hospitality and have gathered around reviews published outside of Southern Italy. It could in fact be said that, all cultural initiatives by mid-level intellectuals that have taken place in the twentieth century in Central and Northern Italy have been characterized by Southernism. This is so because they were strongly influenced by Southern intellectuals: all the reviews of the Florentine intellectual group, *Voce, Unità;* the reviews of the Christian Democrats, like *Azione* of Cesena; the reviews of the young liberals from Emilia and Milano of G. Borelli, like *Patria* of Bologna or *Azione* of Milano; and finally, Gobetti's *La Rivoluzione Liberale*.[35] And the supreme moderators of these initiatives, both politically and intellectually, have been Giustino Fortunato and Benedetto Croce. In a broader sphere than the agrarian bloc, the latter have made certain that the problems of the South would be posed within certain limits and would not become revolutionary. Men of immense culture and intelligence, who emerged from the traditional soil of the South but were tied to European and hence world culture, they possessed all the gifts to satisfy the intellectual needs of the most sincere representative of the cultured youth of the South; to comfort their restless impulses of revolution against existing conditions; to steer them along a middle way of classical serenity of thought and action. The so-called neo-Protestants or

Calvinists have not understood that in Italy, given modern conditions of civilization, a mass religious reform is impossible, the only historically possible reformation has taken place with Benedetto Croce's philosophy. The direction and method of thought has been altered, and a new conception of the world has been constructed, transcending Catholicism and every other mythological religion. In this sense, Benedetto Croce has fulfilled an extremely important "national" function, by having detached the radical intellectuals of the South from the peasant masses and having them participate in national and European culture; and through this culture, he has caused their absorption by the national bourgeoisie and hence by the agrarian bloc.

If, in a certain sense, the *Ordine Nuovo* and the Turin communists can be linked to the intellectual formation to which we have alluded, and if, therefore, they too have felt the intellectual influence of Giustino Fortunato and Benedetto Croce, they nevertheless simultaneously represent a complete break with that tradition and the beginning of a new development, which has already borne fruit and will continue to do so. As has already been said, they have positioned the urban proletariat as modern protagonist of Italian history, and therefore of the Southern question. Having served as intermediaries between the proletariat and certain strata of intellectuals of the left, they have succeeded in modifying, if not completely, then to a notable extent, their mental outlook. When carefully reflected upon, this is a fair representation of Piero Gobetti.[36] He was never a Communist, and would probably never have become one; yet he understood the social and historical position of the proletariat, and could no longer think in abstraction from this element. Through our work together on the paper, Gobetti was placed by us in contact with a living world that he had known before only through the formulas of books. His most striking characteristic was intellectual loyalty, and the total absence of every kind of petty vanity or meanness. He could, therefore, not become convinced of how a whole series of traditional views and manner of thinking about the proletariat were false and unjust. What consequences did these contacts with the proletarian world have on Gobetti? They provided the impulse for a conception which we do not wish to discuss or develop, a conception the large part of which is related to syndicalism and the way of thinking of intellectual syndicalists. In it, the principles of liberalism are projected from the level of individual phenomena to that of mass phenomena. The qualities of excellence and prestige in the lives of individuals are transported over into classes, conceived almost like collective individualities. This conception usually leads, in the intellectuals who share it, to the pure contemplation and recording of its pros and cons; to an odious and foolish position as referees to contests, or as bestowers of prizes and punishments. Gobetti escaped this destiny. He revealed himself to be a great cultural organizer, and he had in this later period a function that must neither be overlooked nor underestimated by the workers. He dug a trench beyond which those groups of honorable and sincere intellectuals who in 1919, 1920 and 1921 felt that the proletariat as a ruling class would be superior to the bourgeoisie, and did not retreat. Some in honesty and good faith, others in bad faith and dishonesty, went about declaring that Gobetti was nothing more than a Communist in disguise; an agent, if not of the Communist Party, then of the Communist group of *Ordine Nuovo*. It is unnecessary even to deny such fatuous rumors. Gobetti and the movement he represented were spontaneous products of the new Italian historical climate, and in this lies their significance and their importance. We have sometimes been reproached by comrades in the Party for not having fought against the current of ideas of *Rivoluzione Liberale*. This absence of conflict seemed to prove the organic relationship, of a Machiavellian type (as they say), between us and Gobetti. We could not fight against Gobetti, because he was carrying out and represented a movement that should not be fought, at least in principle. Not to understand this means not to understand the question of intellectuals and the function that they fulfill in the class struggle. Gobetti served us as a link, as follows: 1. With the intellectuals born on the terrain of capitalist techniques who in 1919-1920 had taken up a left position favorable to the dictatorship of the proletariat; 2. With a series of Southern intellectuals who, due to more complex relationships, posed the Southern question on a terrain different from the traditional one, by introducing into the question the Northern proletariat. Of these latter intellectuals, Guido Dorso is the most complete and interesting figure. Why should we have fought against the *Rivoluzione Liberale* movement? Maybe because it was not made up of pure communists who had accepted our program and our doctrine from A to Z? This question could not be asked, because it would have been paradoxical both politically and historically. Intellectuals develop slowly, much more slowly than any other social group, by their very nature and historical function. They represent the whole of the cultural tradition of a people, seeking to summarize and synthesize all of its history. This is especially true of the old type of intellectual, of the intellectual born of the peasantry. To think it possible that such intellectuals could, *en masse*, break with the entire past and situate themselves wholly on the terrain of a new ideology, is absurd. It is absurd for the intellectuals as a group, and it is possibly absurd for many intellectuals as individuals, despite all their sincere attempts. Now, we are interested in intellectuals as a group, and not only as individuals. It is certainly important for the proletariat that one or more intellectuals, individually, adhere to its program and its doctrine, become enmeshed with the proletariat, and become and feel an integral part of it. The proletariat, as a class, lacks in organizing elements. It does not have its own stratum of intellectuals, and it can only form one very slowly, very painfully, and only after its conquest of State power. But it is also important and useful for a break to occur in the intellectual mass, one that is organic in character and historically characterized; that there be the formation, as a formation of mass, a left tendency, in the modern meaning of the word; in other words, oriented toward the revolutionary proletariat. The alliance between the proletariat and the peasant masses requires this formation. It is required that much more by the alliance between the proletariat and the peasant masses of the South. The proletariat will destroy the Southern agrarian block insofar as it succeeds, through its Party, in organizing increasingly significant masses of poor peasants into autonomous and independent formations. But, its greater or lesser success in this necessary task will depend on its ability to break up the intellectual bloc that is the flexible but very resistant armature of the agrarian bloc. The proletariat has been aided by Piero

Gobetti toward the solution of this task, and we believe that the friends of the now dead Gobetti will continue the work he undertook, even without his guidance. It is a gigantic and difficult enterprise, and because of this all the more worthy of sacrifice (even that of life, as with Gobetti) on the part of those intellectuals (and there are many more than one may believe [28]), both Northerners and Southerners, who have understood that only two social forces are essentially national and bearers of the future: the proletariat and the peasants.

Workers and Peasants

Industrial production must be directly controlled by workers organized by profession; the activity of control must be unified and coordinated through workers' union organizations.[37] The control of industries by the managers (corrupt, venal and irrevocable) of the capitalist State, a form of control that can only lead to a resurgence of committees of industrial mobilization useful only to capitalist parasitism, cannot be conceived as useful to the interests and aspirations of the workers.

The expression "the land to the peasants" must be understood in the sense that agricultural industries and modern farms have to be controlled by organized agricultural workers according to industry

and farm. This means that lands in long-term culti-
vation must be administrated by Councils of poor
peasants from agricultural villages and towns. Agricultural workers, revolutionary peasants and aware
socialists cannot but conceive as useful to their interests and aspirations, to the ends of proletarian educa
tion, indispensable for a Communist republic, the
propaganda for "uncultivated or badly cultivated
lands."[38] This propaganda can result in nothing more
than a dissolution of revolutionary conscience and
faith; it can only result in a monstrous defamation of
socialism.

What does a poor peasant gain by invading
uncultivated or badly cultivated land? Without
machinery, without a home to inhabit on the premis-
es, without credit with which to await harvest time,
without cooperative institutions to purchase the harvest (if by harvest time the peasant hasn't already
hung himself to the strongest shrub, or the least
stunted wild fig tree of his uncultivated land!), thereby saving himself from the hold of usurers; what can
a poor peasant do? He may initially satisfy his
instincts of ownership, satiate his primitive greed for
land. Eventually, realizing that his arms are not
enough to work a land that only dynamite could
break, realizing his need for seed and fertilizers and
for the instruments of labor, he will also realize that
no one will give him these indispensable objects. And

thinking of the future days and nights that he must pass on land without shelter, water – with malaria – the peasant comes to feels his impotence, his solitude, his desperate condition, and becomes a brigand, not a revolutionary; he becomes an assassin of the "rich," and not a fighter for Communism.

This is why revolutionary workers and peasants, and socialists aware of the situation, have not seen their interests and aspirations reflected in parliamentary initiatives for the control of industries and "uncultivated or badly cultivated" lands. They have recognized in these initiatives only parliamentary "idiocy," reformist illusion and opportunism, they have seen counterrevolution. In fact, this parliamentary action could have been useful: it could have served to inform all workers and peasants of exact terms of the industrial and agricultural problem, and of the necessary and sufficient methods with which to resolve it. It could have served to make known to the great mass of Italian peasants that the solution to the agricultural problem could be actualized only by the urban workers of northern Italy, only by a proletarian dictatorship.

The Northern bourgeoisie has subjugated the South of Italy and the Islands, and reduced them to exploitable colonies; by emancipating itself from capitalist slavery, the Northern proletariat will emancipate the Southern peasant masses enslaved to the banks and the parasitic industrialism of the North. The economic and political regeneration of the peasants should not be sought in the division of uncultivated or poorly cultivated lands, but in the solidarity of the industrial proletariat who need, in turn, the solidarity of the peasantry. They have an interest in keeping capitalism from being reborn economically from landed property; that Southern Italy and the Islands do not become a military base for capitalist counter-revolution. By imposing workers' control over industry, the proletariat will reorient industry to the production of agricultural machinery for the peasants, clothing and footwear for the peasants, electrical energy for the peasants; they will prevent industry and banks from exploiting the peasants and subjecting them as slaves to the vaults. By breaking autocracy in the factories, by breaking the oppressive apparatus of the capitalist State and installing a workers' State that will subject the capitalists to the law of useful labor, the workers will break all the chains that hold the peasants to their poverty and desperation. By installing a workers' dictatorship, by taking hold of the industries and banks, the proletariat will turn the enormous power of the state apparatus to the aid of the peasants in their struggle against the landowners, against the elements, against misery. The proletariat will provide peasants with credit, set up cooperatives, guarantee security of person and property against looters, and carry out public works of reclamation and irrigation. It will do all this because it is in its interest to increase agricultural production, because it is in its interest to have and conserve the solidarity of the peasant masses, because it is in its interest to orient industrial production to useful work that will promote peace between the city and the countryside, between North and South.

In this sense, knowledgeable workers and peasants require socialist parliamentary action to address the achievement of revolutionary education among the masses, the unification of sentiments and aspiration of the masses to the scope of the Communist program; to propagate incessantly the conviction that the present problems of industrial and agricultural economy can only be resolved outside of the Parliament, against the Parliament, by a workers' State.

Letter for the Foundation of *L'Unità*

To the Executive Committee of the Italian Communist Party

September 12, 1923

Dear Comrades,

During the last session, the President. decided that Italy should have a workers' daily. Edited by the EC, it would also favour contributions from the third internationalists who are excluded by the Socialist Party.[39]

I believe that it will be useful and necessary, given the present situation in Italy, that the paper be compiled in such a way as to ensure its legal existence for the longest time possible. Therefore, not only should the paper not carry any signs of party affiliation, but it must be edited so that its actual dependency on our party not be too apparent. It will have to be a paper of the left, of the workers' left, that has remained faithful to the program and the tactics of the class struggle. It will publish the acts and discussions of our party, as it will also do with the acts and discussions of the anarchists, republicans and unionists, and it will give its objective opinion as something held above the struggle and offering a "scientific" point of view. I understand that it is not easy to fix everything in a written program, but what is important is not to set down a written program, rather to ensure the party itself of an historically dominant position in the field of workers of the left. In such a manner it (the party) will have a legal tribune that will allow it to reach the most distant masses continually and systematically.

Communists and Serratians will contribute to the paper openly, in other words by signing the articles with visible elements according to a political plan that will take account month by month, and week by week, of the general situation of the country and of the relationships that develop among Italian social forces.[40] We will have to be careful of the Serratians, who will tend to transform the paper into an organ of factional struggle against the leaders of the Socialist Party. We will have to be stern in this matter and prevent any degeneration. The polemic will necessarily take place, but in political spirit and not as a sect or within such limitations. We will have to be careful not to create an "economic" situation for Serrati who, being unemployed, will be proposed by his comrades to act as editor. Serrati will contribute with and without a byline; his signed articles will have to conform to certain limits and the unsigned ones will have to be accepted by our EC. It will be necessary to initiate polemics of principle with the socialists, or better with the socialist spirit of Serrati, Maffi and others. This will be useful in consolidating the Communist conscience of the masses, and preparing the party for unity and homogeneity that will be necessary after the fusion, so as to avoid a re-occurrence of the chaotic situation of 1920.

As a title, I propose *L'Unità* pure and simple. It will have a meaning for the workers and a more general meaning because I believe that, after the decision of the executive on the workers' and peasants' government, we will have to emphasize the importance of the Southern Question[41]; in other words, in the question that poses the problem of the relationship between workers and peasants, not only as a problem of class, but also, and especially, as a problem of territory, as one of the characteristics of the national question.[42] Personally, I believe that the password "workers' and peasants' government" must be adapted to the Italian situation in the following manner: "Federal Republic of workers and peasants." I am not certain whether the present moment is favorable to this; I believe, however, that the situation that Fascism is creating, and the corporate and protectionist politics of the confederalists, will carry our own party to this password. To this purpose, I am preparing a report for you to discuss and examine. If useful, after a certain number of issues, we could initiate a polemic in the pages of the paper using pseudonyms to see what its repercussions might be around the country, and in the ranks of the left of the popularists and democrats who represent the real tendencies of the peasant class and have always had the password of local autonomy and decentralization within their program. If you accept the proposed title *L'Unità,* you will make space for the resolution of these problems and the title will be a guarantee against degeneration into autonomism and against reactionary attempts to give tendentious and mysterious interpretations to the campaigns that we might undertake. Besides, I believe that the regime of the Soviets, with its political centralization given by the Communist Party, and its administrative decentralization, and its colorization of the local popular forces, will find an excellent ideological preparation in the password: Federal Republic of workers and peasants.

Communist greetings,

Gramsci

Antonio Gramsci

Born in Sardegna and educated on the Italian mainland, Antonio Gramsci (1891-1937) is among the leading thinkers of the twentieth century. As a Marxist, Gramsci is a figure who has come to represent the open mindedness of Marxism; to emphasize the difference between those who have made of Marxism a dogma and those who have carried on its open ended research. He helped found the Italian Communist Party (PCI) in 1921 and was its Secretary. Gramsci was also the founder and editor of the newspapers *L'ordine nuovo* and *L'unità,* the latter being the organ of the PCI.

On the mainland of Italy, in Turin, Gramsci quickly became involved in the workers' movement. One of his principal areas of concentration, both on the practical and theoretical levels, was the relationship between the Italian North and its Southern regions and Islands. It was within that framework, established in the earlier *The Southern Question* (1926) that much of the writing contained in his *Prison Notebooks* developed. Written during his incarceration by Mussolini's Fascists from 1926 to

1937, the *Notebooks* have become a major point of reference not only in Italian cultural politics, but also throughout the world in their usefulness for the analysis of national situations. By offering an enlarged view, comprehensive not only of class but also of cultural relationships as these condition economic structures, Gramsci's concepts have been used, most notably, within the parameters of Liberation Theology, by members of the "Birmingham Cultural Studies Collective" and the "Indian Subaltern Studies Group."

I would briefly like to note that, while many have recognized Gramsci's importance for the study of race and ethnicity, a certain distance remains in relation to his work when it comes to recognizing that his analysis of the North/South situation was also a critique of constructions of race and ethnic differences as found in the work of positivist anthropologists, followers of Lombroso's systems of categorization. I would add that recognition of such subtleties, within what has been cast as a generalized category of "whiteness," may in fact be a useful way to undermine that category from within. The failure to acknowledge this aspect of Gramsci's writings may indeed be related to a perceived necessity to maintain, at least on a subliminal level and within situations such as the U.S.A., an image of Italy as a homogeneous nation without racial or ethnic difference. This, however, precludes the possibility of understanding the racialized foundation of Italian nationhood, the very basis from which Gramsci thought emerged.

Bibliography

Alcaro, Mario. *Sull'identità merdionale: Forme di una cultura mediterranea.* Saggi. Torino: Bollati Boringhieri, 1999.

Bassolino, Antonio. *La repubblica delle città.* Interventi/31. Roma: Donzelli, 1996.

Cassano, Franco. *Il pensiero meridiano.* Saggitari Laterza 94. Bari: Laterza, 1996.

D'Amato, Antonio. *Intervista di Roberto Napoletano. Mezzogiorno, risorsa nascosta: Come e dove attuare una politica di sviluppo per univer il paese. Biblioteca di economia.* Milano: Sperling and Kupfer Editori, 1997.

Piperno, Franco. *Elogio dello spirito pubblico meridionale: genius loci e individuo sociale.* Le esche 11. Roma: Manifestolibri, 1997.

Introduction

1. I have annotated this translation of *The Southern Question* to provide some perhaps useful information regarding some of the most important individuals and elements mentioned in its pages that often go uncommented.

2. PCI = Italian Communist Party, Antonio Gramsci was among its founders (1921) and was its Secretary. Though the "Fascist march on Rome" has now taken on a quasi-mythological status, Mussolini's ascent to power was made possible by an historical alliance between then Prime Minister Giolitti's Liberals, its conservative opposition, and the *Partito Nazionale Fascista.* The story of the "march on Rome" is just that, a story meant as much to embellish Fascist history as to veil the collaboration and involvement of other interested parties.

3. Antonio Gramsci. *Quaderni del carcere, edizione critica dell'Istituto Gramsci. A cura di Valentino Gerratana* (Torino: Einaudi, 1975).

4. Edward Said. *Culture and Imperialism* (New York: Knopf, 1994).

5. Journal founded by Gramsci in 1919. Began as a weekly, it eventually became the daily organ of Turin's factory councils.

6. Antonio Gramsci. *Il Risorgimento edizione "I piccoli."* (Roma: Riuniti, 1991).

7. In *States of Emergency: Cultures of Revolt in Italy from 1968 to 1978* (N.Y.: Verso, 1990), Robert Lumley provides an account of Southern Italian migrant workers within the Northern industrial complex. See in particular "Turin Events – Southerners Revolt," pp. 209-214.

8. Piero Bevilacqua. *Breve storia dell'Italia meridionale dall'Ottocento a oggi.* Saggi. Storia e scienze sociali. (Roma: Donzelli, 1993).

9. I quote from a speech on the Southern Question presented in Palermo on February 21, 1971. A portion of this speech was then used as the introduction to a pamphlet publication of Gramsci's *The Southern Question* given as a gift with the weekly *Avvenimenti,* June 1993.

10. The *Lega's* views of African, Middle Eastern, and Eastern European immigrants to Italy is similarly biased.

11. Tobias Abse. "The Triumph of the Leopard." New Left Review. no. 199 (1993): 18. This is a telling statement as far as Abse is concerned. In fact, the belief of a corrupt South continues to dominate in the minds of most non-Southerners, Italian or foreign. While this is a view undoubtably conditioned by the presence of the Mafia, *ndrangheta* and Camorra, it retains that positivist tendency to generalize along pseudo-social or scientific lines in its reference to Southerners, be they involved in criminal activities or not. Another article of note that further illustrates the staying power of positivist depictions of Southerners is Frank Viviano's article on the Lombard League: "The Fall of Rome" in *Mother Jones.* Sept./Oct. (1993): 36-40. The Italian elections of June 20, 1993, during which the stronghold of the Christian Democrats and their Socialist cronies was undone, provides a picture of the "two Italies" that in some respects has remained unchanged since the unification of the country. During the course of these elections, the result

of an electoral reform referendum that took place in April 1993, the Lombard League swept the North, and the South redefined itself on the Left. Tobias Abse's analysis of the referendum, in "The Triumph of the Leopard: How Italians Have Been Cheated" (*New Left Review,* No. 199 [1993]), makes clear that the intended results were to overturn the old order of politics, which, with the Christian Democrats at the helm, had dominated Italy since the establishment of the Republic during the post WWII years. Appropriately, Abse opens his article with a quote from Tommaso di Lampedusa's historical novel *Il gattopardo* (*The Leopard*), which reflects the Sicilian author's verdict on the meaning of unification for the South: "If we want things to stay as they are, things will have to change." The referendum on electoral reform made for odd partnerships in support of reform. The *Lega* joined the PDS (Democratic Party of the Left, formerly the PCI), the DC (Christian Democrats), and the PSI (Socialist Party) in support of the "Yes" vote. While the MSI (*Movimento Sociale Italiano*, the neo-fascist party) and *Rifondazione Comunista* (breakaways from the reformed PCI) and a group of smaller parties of the left were in support of the "No" vote.

12. Umberto Brindani & Daniele Vimercati, eds.. *Il pensiero Bossi: 1979-1993 La prima raccolta di scritti e discorsi per capire chi è e che cosa vuole davvero l'uomo più temuto d'Italia.* Panorama documenti 1993.

13. See my "Bound by Distance: Italian-Canadian Writing as Decontextualized Subaltern" in *Voices in Italian Americana,* 3, 2 (1992): 15-30.

14. A bipolar and simple dichotomy would be inadequate to describe the situation. In *The Southern Question* for example, Gramsci himself envisioned the South as three politically homogeneous regions on the social and class levels but nevertheless different by civil and cultural traditions. Furthermore, in the notes for the project that will be his *Prison Notebooks,* Gramsci notes, as the title for "argument 9," *"La quistione meridionale e la quistione delle isole."* In addition, there are considerations of three distinct "southern ques-

tions" addressed in paragraph 47 of notebook 14, and paragraph 26 of notebook 19 (Giuseppe Fiori, *Gramsci Togliatti Stalin,* [Bari: Laterza, 1991] 193). A useful introduction to Gramsci's concept of "national popular" is to be found in David Forgacs' "National-popular: genealogy of a concept," in *The Cultural Studies Reader,* Simon During ed., (New York: Routledge, 1993), 177-190.

15. Stuart Hall. "Gramsci's relevance for the study of race and ethnicity" *Journal of Communication Inquiry,* 10, 2: 5-27.

The Southern Question

1. This manuscript was misplaced during the period of Gramsci's arrest and was later found among the papers that had been abandoned in Gramsci's apartment by Camilla Ravera. It was published in January 1930 in *Stato Operaio,* in Paris. The following note accompanied the publication: "This piece is unfinished and its author would most likely have returned to it at a later date. It is being reproduced here without any changes, as the best document of communist political thought, incomparably deep, strong, original and rich with the most far reaching developments." From *Duemila pagine di Gramsci* a.c. di G. Ferrata e N. Gallo (Il Saggiatore, 1964).

2. *Quarto Stato* was an important neo-Marxian journal founded and directed by Carlo Rosselli with Pietro Nenni in Milano in 1926. A staunch anti-Fascist of Jewish background, Rosselli was indicted for crimes against the state in 1927. Imprisoned on the island of Lipari, he made an adventurous escape with Emilio Lussu and Fausto Nitti in 1929 and settled in France. There he published *Socialismo liberale* (Liberal Socialism), written on the island, in 1930. From France he helped keep alive the anti-Fascist struggle throughout Europe. With the outbreak of civil war in Spain he joined as a fighter against Franco's Fascists. During that period he wrote essays that were posthumously published as

Oggi in Spagna domani in Italia (Today in Spain, Tomorrow in Italy). In 1936 he was wounded and retired to France to recover; he and his brother Nello were murdered by French assassins working on behalf of Mussolini's Fascists. Bertolucci's film *The Conformist* is based on the events surrounding Rosselli's assassination. *Ulenspiegel* was the pseudonym of Tommaso Fiore, a correspondent for *Rivoluzione Liberale*.

3. Guido Dorso (1892-1947) was an anti-fascist political writer and revolutionary interventionist. During the WWI period, he was a correspondent for *Popolo d'Italia,* a periodical with strong "southernist" inflections. He and his publisher Piero Gobetti came to represent the most progressive wing of Italian liberalism in post World War I Italy. In his *La rivoluzione meridionale (The Southern Revolution)* (1925), Dorso offers an organic exposition of the South's backwardness. His analysis is based on the liberal-radical critique of the Southern leading class and its re-enforcement by the Risorgimento period.

4. *L'Ordine Nuovo (The New Order)* was the theoretical and political organ of the socialist left in Turin; it was founded by Antonio Gramsci in 1919. Originally published as a weekly, it became a daily in January 1921, when the Italian Communist Party was about to be founded. The publication dedicated much space to anti-reformist discussions, to theoretical and practical aspects that emerged from the October revolution, and to discussions engendered within the Communist International. It published articles by Lenin, Bucharin, Gorki, Radek and others, as well as delineating the Gramscian program of the industrial councils.

5. For the complete text see the accompanying piece, "Workers and Peasants."

6 . This is a reference to Gaetano Salvemini who, when he left the PSI in 1910, described his political views as "concretism." This term refers to the tendency to see the Southern Question in its fragments, and attempting to solve each problem individually, thereby dissolving the political urgency of the problem. Salvemini founded the daily *L'Unità*.

7. Giustino Fortunato (1848-1932) was a liberal conservative whose name was closely tied to issues regarding the southern question, which he approached in terms different from the traditional view of a rich and fertile land ruined by its inhabitants. In his *Il Mezzogiorno e lo Stato italiano (The South and the Italian State)* (1911) he considers geological and climatic aspects of the region that according to him defined the South's natural poverty. An anti-fascist, he was under constant surveillance by the Fascists, but was not personally persecuted.

Gaetano Salvemini (1873-1957), a slow-to-develop socialist and Marxist, became an important collaborator of the periodical *Voce.* He broke from that group in 1911, as a result of the Lybian war, which he opposed. As time moved on he distanced himself from the Socialist party. Active member of the antifascist group *Circolo di cultura,* he founded the activist journal *Non Mollare* in 1925. Arrested and brought under indictment for this activity, he was given provisional liberty and expatriated to Paris. In answer to his resignation from the Florentine Atheneum, Mussolini revoked his Italian citizenship. In 1933 he left for the U.S.A. and a teaching position at Harvard. After a long expatriate struggle against Fascism, he finally returned to Italy in 1950 to reclaim his professorship in Florence.

Eugenio Azimonti, an agrarian, was a contributor to *L'Unità* and *La rivoluzione liberale* papers, in 1919 he published *Il Mezzogiorno agrario qual'è.*

Arturo Labriola (1873-1959), was an economist and political activist. Following his participation in the Socialist movements of 1898 he was forced into exile in Switzerland. On his return to Naples, he became head of the most radical wing of the Socialist party. Minister of Labor in 1920-21 in the Giolitti government, Labriola was once again forced into exile with the advent of Fascism. In 1937 he returned to Italy, but refrained from all political activity until the fall of Mussolini. Among his more important works are *Karl Marx's Value Theory* (1899); *Capitalism* (1910); *A History of Ten Years: 1899-1909* (1910).

8. This conception of the South, as the ball and chain that arrests national development, has continued to be used in reference to the South as a backward region that absorbs the surplus capital of the more economically advanced Northern region. Most recently, Giorgio Bocca has used this expression verbatim in order to describe the perceived threat by which the ball and chain South will drag Italy into the Third World (*La disUnità d'Italia [Italian disUnity]* Rizzoli, 1990).

9. These positivists were strongly influenced by the work of the famed criminologist Lombroso. Their writings emphasized the "racial" inferiority of Southerners. Particularly notable are A. Niceforo's *Italiani del Nord e italiani del sud (Northern Italians and Southern Italians)* (1901) and *L'Italia barbara contemporanea (Contemporary Barbarian Italy)* (1898); and Cesare Lombroso's *In Calabria* (1862).

10. The repression battles of "brigand" rebellions in the South in post-unification Italy were particularly bloody. Many stories circulated among soldiers about the brutality and savagery of Southerners. Though tens of thousands of "brigands" and their collaborators were killed, jailed or exiled, most of the rumors placed the blame for atrocities at the feet of the "brigands." Most influential among the stories told were those recounting episodes of cannibalism, in which captured soldiers were tortured, flayed and devoured.

11. This is a reference to the alliances that the Turin Communists were able to forge among workers in the North, some of whom included immigrants from the South and the Islands. It is also a reference to the activity of the Communists at the meeting for the formation of a regional bloc which will be approached in the pages that follow.

12. Filippo Turati (1877-1932) was founder of the journal *Critica Social (Social Critique)*. He attempted to unite the humanitarian tendencies of the most advanced points of bouregoisie with the labor movement. In 1891 he helped found the Workers Party. As such, Turati's most useful contribution is obviously the insertion of the concrete problems of the working classes in the process of development of the

democratic-liberal state, divorced from a Marxist agenda. In 1892 the Workers Party became the Socialist Party. Under Fascism, he was forced into exile to Paris.

Claudio Treves (1869-1933) was a contributor to *Critica Sociale* and a close friend and collaborator of Turati's. In 1922 he moved, with the right wing of the Socialist Party, to form the PSU (Unitarian Socialist party).

Ludovico D'Aragona (1876-1961) was member of the Socialist Party from its beginnings in 1892. He suffered continuous arrests until he fled to France and then Switzerland in 1895 and 1898 respectively. Elected as a Socialist deputy in 1919, with Fascism's rise he retired into a private life. In 1947 he joined the Democratic Socialist party that formed as a splinter of the Socialist Party. He became a well-known minister of various portfolios during De Gasperi's various cabinets.

13. Mussolini was director of *Avanti!* and, at that time, there was a certain convergence of thought between Mussolini and Salvemini in their critique of reformist socialists.

14. Autonomous Movement of WWI Veterans was founded in 1919 by Emilio Lussu. This organization played a similar, but autonomous, part in politics to Mazzini's Action Party of 1853. It seems that it was loosely tied to an idea for the formation of a Federal Mediterranean State that would have included Catalunia, the Baleares, Corsica and Sardegna, Sicily and Candia. (Gramsci, *Quaderni del Carcere,* pg. 768)

15. The counter-presentation caused a great stir for its proposal to forego the formation of a regional bloc for one between Sardinian workers and "the revolutionary workers of the mainland." It was quite a task for the Communists to highlight that alliance as being more important than the regional rhetoric used to stir people's feelings and sentiments living away from their land and relatives.

16. The Sassari Brigade, called to Turin during the occupation of the factories in 1920, had been used for repression of the August 1917 rebellion on the part of the Turin proletariat for bread, and against the war. It was used again in the hope that the memory of the initial encounter would still be fresh

and serve to foment even more antagonism between the two sides. The Brigade was mostly made of Sardinians (hence the name Sassari, which is a city in Sardegna and is the point of origin of its formation). It was a military formation, part of the Armed Forces. As such it was primarily under the direction of Northern authorities, giving a sort of exploitative continuity to the relationship between the Piedmontese and the Sardinians, the latter having been under the former's rule prior to unification.

17. The Socialist newspaper founded in Rome in 1896. *Avanti's* directors included L. Bissolati, E. Ferri, C. Treves and B. Mussolini. The Fascist regime ordered its suppression in 1926, but it continued to publish in France, and re-emerged during the resistance in Italy.

18. The formation of the Sardinian Action Party was influenced by the presence of military men who had been involved in wars that ranged from the war with Lybia in 1911 to WWI, to the suppression of insurgents at home.

19. Rebellions of the Sicilian Fasci and of the Lunigiana of 1894, fiercely repressed by Prime Minister Crispi. 1898 brought a fierce series of revolts in all Italy. Particularly strong in Milano, they were put down with deadly force by General Bava Beccaris. The Sicilian Fasci were organizations made up of workers and peasants in defense of their interests. Founded in 1891, they developed all over Sicily and were under the leadership of N. Barbato and G. De Felice-Giuffrica.

20. Syndicalism was a revisionist movement that achieved its most effectual expression in France, with Sorel, and in Italy with Arturo Labriola, Enrico Leone and Paolo Orano. The syndicalist movement was eventually largely incorporated into Fascism.

21. Enrico Corradini (1865-1931) was an influential nationalist intellectual, a theorist of what Gramsci referred to as "national socialism," or the transfer of class struggle onto a struggle of nations. His nationalist ideology found free circulation in the journal *Il Regno* (The Kingdom), founded by him in 1903. Among his novels, in which the myth of

"the proletarian nation" sending its masses out to colonize the world is clearly evident, are La patria lontana (*The Distant Homeland,* 1910) and La guerra lontàna (TheDistant War, 1911). Among the strongest supporters of this ideology were Giovanni Pascoli and Gabriele D'Annunzio.

22. A Florentine literary and political journal published between 1908 and 1916.

23. For more on Mussolini see Denis Mack Smith *Mussolini* (New York: Knopf, 1982), and Martin Blinkhorn's *Mussolini and Fascist Italy* (London: Routledge, 1994), second edition. The most obvious oversight in the latter (to put it diplomatically) is the total absence of any mention of the formation of the Italian Communist Party and its founder, Antonio Gramsci.

24. Revolutionary movement of the Marche and Romagna regions in 1914, ignited by a Police massacre of the participants in a popular meeting, is indicative of social tensions of the day and of popular opposition to the war.

25. Giorgio Sidney Sonnino (1847-1922) was an active diplomat and politico of Jewish and English background, Sonnino shared view with France and Britain that a weakened but not destroyed Austro-Hungarian empire, nevertheless, had to become secondary in order to act in Italy's benefit.

   Antonio Salandra (1853-1931). A deputy of the conservative center right in 1866. Collaborator to Sonnino's *Rassegna settimanale (Weekly Review)*, he also was part of the latter's short-lived governments as minister of finance and treasury. In 1923 Mussolini appointed him as Italian representative to the Society of Nations. He was elected senator in 1928.

26. Francesco Nitti (1868-1953). Adherent to Giolitti until the latter's fall. Exiled in 1924 to Switzerland and then France, where he participated in the organization of anti-fascist groups, and the writing of antifascist literature. In 1943 he was arrested by the Nazis and deported. On his return to Italy he founded, with Croce, Orlando and Bonomi, the *Unione democratica nazionale (National Democratic Union)*.

   Francesco Crispi (1819-1901) was a Republican whose

ties with Mazzini were very strong. He became closely associated with the organization of the Mille expedition of 1860 that was to unite the peninsula. Elected as deputy in 1861, he was on the extreme left and was considered among the most intransingent defender of republican views. In 1864 he broke with Mazzini and accepted monarchy as an option. In 1887 he became president of the council and took on an aggressive foreign policy. Strongly and aggressively colonial in aspect, Crispi achieved the colonization of Eritrea while plunging the country into economic and social strife. Forced to resign in 1891, he was nevertheless asked to reform a government when rebellions broke out in Sicily and Lunigiana, A state of seige was declared and the upheaval quelled militaristically. In 1894 when the Socialist party was declared illegal due to its sympathizing with the rebellions, the general elections in 1895 gave Crispi an absolute majority. The following year, with the military failure at Adua, he was forced to resign for good.

27.   The center of reformist socialism for some time, Reggio Emilia is a the heart of Italy's "Red Triangle," a perennially Left region.

28.   Prampolini was a leader of the PSU (reformist socialist party) and editor of the party publication, *La Giustizia (Justice)*. The original pun is *"nordici e sudici,"* playing on the opposition of Northeners and Southerners (nord=north and sud=south). While *"nordici"* does in fact mean Northeners, *"sudici"* does not mean Southerners but is the plural of "filthy" *(sudicio); therefore* my translation of *"sudici"* as sowtherners.

29.   Benedetto Croce (1866-1952) was a philosopher and historian of international renown. Many biographies are available on Croce. Among his many important publications is *La letteratura della nuova Italia (Literature of the New Italy)*.

30.   Duke Giovanni Colonna di Cesarò was a representative of Social Democracy, the political entity of large Southern land owners.

31.   See Franchetti's *Condizioni economiche ed amministrative delle provincie napoletane (Economic and Administrative*

Conditions of the Neapolitan Provinces, 1875) and his joint endeavour with Sonnino, *La Sicilia nel 1876 (Sicily in 1876,* 1877).

32. Gramsci reflects on his own heritage in his letters: "I myself have no race: my father is of recent Albanian origin (his family left Epirius before or during the wars of 1821 and quickly italianized itself); my grandmother was a Gonzalez, a descendant of some Italian-Spanish family of Southern Italy." *Lettere dal carcere (Letters from Prison)*(Torino: Einaudi, 1965) (506-507).

33. Gramsci's use of "middle culture" and "medium intellectuals" is loosely adaptable to the term middle class.

34. Benedetto Croce's critical review of culture, founded in 1903.

35. *La Rivoluzione liberale* was a journal founded and edited by Piero Gobetti from 1922 to 1925.

36. Piero Gobetti (1901-1926), man of politics and letters. In 1922 he founded *Rivoluzione Liberale (Liberal Revolution)*. He considered the Risorgimento a failure for its having been the expression of the will of a few, and therefore tainted by a sense of paternalism. He fought against Fascism and was forced into exile in France. It is important to note that Gramsci paid great attention and tribute to Gobetti. He recognized the latter's contribution in having "understood the social and historical position of the proletariat." In many ways, Gramsci's drawing near to Gobetti's work is illustrative of the concept of alliances and the function and formation of intellectuals that thread through *The Southern Question*.

37. From *L'Ordine Nuovo,* January 3, 1920.

38. This is the origin of the polemic regarding land that is addressed in *The Southern Question*. Reformists, and portions of the government at the time, supported the proposal of transferring to the peasants "unused or badly cultivated lands."

39. From *Rinascita,* cultural journal of PCI (Italian Communist Party), Feb. 8, 1964.

40. Followers of Serrati, who led a splinter group from the PSI.

41. *Unità (Unity)*, as is clear throughout the letter, for Gramsci

means not only the unity to be sought between workers and peasants, but also among socialist forces.

42. The importance of this letter goes beyond its declaration of the need for unity among socialist forces to stress the import of the Southern Question. Within the landscape of the *Southern Question* there emerges yet another consideration of its centrality as an issue, which is stated in Gramsci's emphasis of "territorial" concerns. This expansion of the Southern Question into a national concern, along with the proposed alliance of Northern workers and Southern peasants, provides a mode by which to translate the password "wokers and peasants' government" to the particular Italian situation.

MIX
Paper from
responsible sources
FSC® C100212

Printed by Imprimerie Gauvin
Gatineau, Québec